TOURIST GUIDE

USEFUL INFORMATION • MAP

KOS

• DESCRIPTION OF THE CITY • SIGHTS • MONUMENTS
• EXCURSIONS
• LIST OF HOTELS

TEXT: ELENI PALASKA-PAPASTATHI

CONTENTS

INTRODUCTION 9
GEOGRAPHICAL OUTLINE 11
HISTORICAL OUTLINE 12
HIPPOKRATES 25
POPULAR CULTURE AND TRADITION 30
MODERN LIFE ON THE ISLAND 33
TOUR OF THE ISLAND 40
THE MODERN CITY 45
SIGHTS IN THE CITY 52
EXCURSIONS 79
THE ASKLEPIEION 79
AROUND THE TOWN 84
ASPHENDIOU 85
PYLI 87
ANTIMACHEIA 90
KARDAMAINA 99
KEPHALOS 102
GENERAL INFORMATION 110
NISYROS 114
ACCOMMODATION 122
MAP 126

The verdant island of Kos lies between
Kalymnos and Nisyros at the south-east corner
of the Greek Archipelago - the Aegean islands -
thrust like a wedge into the intricate
complexity of the coastline of Asia Minor.
Its fame as the birthplace of Hippokrates,
the father of medical science, far transcends
the narrow borders of Greece and resounds throughout
the entire world. Fame...but also unrivalled natural beauty,
archaeological remains that attest to its rich past,
a superb tourist infrastructure, easy access - by sea and air -
and regular connections with the Aegean islands,
a gentle climate, traditional villages in the interior
of the island, endless sandy beaches with azure sea,
a variety of interests, artistic events, popular festivals,
a cosmopolitan environment and also opportunities
for peaceful relaxation in areas off the beaten track -
these are the main attractions for the thousands
who visit the beautiful island.
The newly arrived visitor is immediately captivated
by the city of Kos, with its imposing Venetian castle,
built by the Knights of Rhodes, and its wide streets
flanked by tall palm trees. The Asklepieion,
built in superb natural surroundings,
is equally impressive, with the ruins of the temples
of Asklepios and Apollo Kyparissios.
Nature-lovers and those seeking peace and quiet
will find authentic traditional villages
to which they can withdraw.
No-one is disappointed on Kos.
Kos is an island for all tastes and - because
of its mild climate - for all seasons!

GEOGRAPHICAL OUTLINE

Kos is the third largest island in the Dodecanese, after Rhodes and Karpathos. It has an area of 290 square kilometres, and approximately 113 kilometres of coastline, and lies at the entrance to the Kerameikos Gulf in Asia Minor, south of Kalymnos and Pserimos and north of Nisyros. It has an elongated shape and consists mostly of plains, with the mountains, Dikaios (846 m.) and Sympetros, confined to the south-eastern area of the island. In addition to the broad bay of Kephalos on the east side, and the bay of Kos, where the main port of the island is located, the coastline is fragmented by small, mainly sandy inlets that create the promontories of Skandari, Psalidi, Ayios Phokas, Krikelo and Drepano.

The island has an abundance of water and healing springs. The soil is fertile and the climate mild and healthy and there are many olive groves, vineyards, vegetable gardens and orchards producing citrus fruit. Some of the inhabitants make a living as fishermen and farmers, in cottage industries and in shipping, but the majority are employed in tourism, which has grown in leaps and bounds in recent decades and makes a decisive contribution to the local income: of the islands in the Dodecanese, Kos is second only to Rhodes in terms of tourist development and the influx of foreign exchange. Together with Nisyros and the surrounding barren islands, it forms the administrative province of Kos within the county of the Dodecanese. The island is populated by about 20,000 inhabitants.

Below: the small harbour near the village of Pyli.

HISTORICAL OUTLINE

There is a rich store of myths connected with the beautiful island of Kos. According to one legend, it was here that the Titans Koios and Kynnes took refuge after their defeat by the Olympian gods. The giant Polybotes, too, hid himself on Kos when pursued by the sea-god Poseidon; he was unable to escape the sea-god's wrath, however, and was crushed by an enormous rock torn from the island by Poseidon. Another legend links Kos with the hero Herakles who, while carrying out one of his labours, was shipwrecked in the sea off the island and sought refuge on its soil for himself and his companions.

Originally, Kos was called Kynnis, a name deriving from that of the Titan Kynnes in the myth mentioned above. It was later known as Karis, after the Karians, who came from the mainland opposite, and as Meropis, after the mythical king of the island, Merops; at this time the islanders were known as Meropes. It owes its present name to Koos, or Kos, the daughter of King Merops II.

Scholars have attempted, by interpreting the wealth of archaeological finds on the island, to establish the thread connecting its mythology with its history - an endeavour in which they have been aided by literary references from Homer to Strabo. In the light of all this evidence, it is beyond doubt that Kos has been continuously occupied ever since the prehistoric period. The earliest inhabitants are thought to have been the Pelasgoi, who came from mainland Greece and Asia Minor, opposite. The passage of the Pelasgoi is attested by the `Pelasgian' remains discovered at Ayios Phokas and Palaioskala. The Pelasgians were followed

Right: part of the harbour excavations.
Below: the temple of Asklepios.

by the Karians and the Leleges, tribes from Asia Minor that were incorporated into the population of the island. Later, Kos entered into alliance with the Minoans of Crete, who were the masters of the entire Aegean, and was influenced by their civilisation. This was followed by influences from the Mycenaean civilisation, as is clear from the remains of a Mycenaean settlement on the island. The Mycenaeans were succeeded by the Phoenicians, the Achaeans and, finally, the Dorians, who became the predominant element in the population, and whose dialect became the dominant language.

HISTORICAL OUTLINE

References in the Iliad make it clear that Kos took part in the Trojan War with thirty ships under Pheidippos and Antiphon, the grandsons of Herakles. The constitution of the island was originally a monarchy, which was later replaced by an oligarchy (8th-7th century BC). An event of decisive importance for the history of the island occurred in the 7th century BC: the foundation of the `Dorian Hexapolis' (union of six cities), consisting of Kos, Ialysos, Kameiros, Lindos -the three leading cities on the nearby island of Rhodes - and Knidos and Halikarnassos, on the Asia Minor coast opposite. The religious centre of the Hexapolis was the sanctuary of Apollo Triopios on the promontory of the same name (now Kavos Krios). This alliance formed a powerful federal state, to use modern terminology, which, in addition to its purely military-defensive character, also had political overtones, as well as economic and religious ties. The Hexapolis was thus able to dominate the surrounding area of the Aegean and each of the member-cities of which it was formed reached great heights of prosperity. Trade, shipping, industry and pottery-production all developed on Kos at this period and the arts and letters

flourished, while the first steps were taken and the foundations laid of the science of medicine, through the activities of Hippokrates.

In the 6th century BC, the constitution of the island became a democracy, on the model of the Solonian democracy at Athens. In the 5th century BC, Kos, in common with the other Aegean islands, the Greek cities on the coast of Asia Minor, and the cities of mainland Greece, became the object of Persian aggression. It took part in the struggle against the Persians and was initially conquered, along with the other Greeks. Later, however, after the expulsion of the Persian forces, it became part of the First Athenian Confederacy. Another destructive war was to call a temporary halt to the island's steady advance: the Peloponnesian War (431-404), fought between the Athenians and the Spartans. During this conflict, Kos naturally took the side of the Athenian allies and, having been defeated by the enemy in 411 BC, was captured and suffered severe pillaging and destruction. Later, a civil war broke out on the island

Part of the Asklepieion.

between the democrats and the oligarchs, after which a major earthquake levelled the capital, Astypalaia. The island was able to recover, however, and in the 4th century BC was flourishing once more, especially after the foundation in 366 BC of the new city of Kos, on the site of the modern capital at the north-east end of the island. Kos once more became one of the most important naval and trading powers in the Aegean. Along with its neighbour, Rhodes, it became a member of the Second Athenian Confederacy. The two islands later broke free of the influence of Athens and, when the Macedonians became the major power in Greece, first under Philip and then under Alexander the Great, they aligned themselves on the Macedonian side. Hippokrates, whose teaching laid the foundations of medical science, was born, lived and was active on Kos (460-357 BC). After his death, the Asklepieion was founded on the island and acquired great fame in Greece and the whole of the then known world, being visited by thousands of sick people. The sacred precinct was a place of asylum, and every five years the 'Great Asklepieia' were held there - official, pan-Hellenic artistic and athletic contests in which representatives of all the Greek cities took part. Kos thus became a pan-Hellenic cultural and historical centre. A number of outstanding doctors offered their services after the death of Hippokrates: Erasipatros, Nikas, Dexippos and Kritsodemos. The last-named accompanied Alexander the Great on his campaign and saved his life, when it was endangered in India. Epicharmos, the founder of Sicilian Comedy, was also

Left: ruins of the large temple of Asklepios.

from Kos, as was the poet Herondas, Xenokritos, the scholiast on the writings of Hippokrates, and others. Another who lived on Kos was the lyric poet Theokritos, who was born in Sicily and died at Alexandria (310-250 BC), and was famous for his bucolic `Idylls'. In the Hellenistic period, the island formed part of the kingdom of Antigonos and continued to prosper (323 BC).

Kos later became an ally of Rome and eventually fell under Roman suzerainty, as did the rest of Greece, though retaining a relative degree of autonomy, thanks to which it continued to be a naval power. It was in 82 BC that the Romans expelled Mithridates, who had occupied the island since 88 BC, and made Kos and the neighbouring islands a Roman province with its capital at Rhodes.

HISTORICAL OUTLINE

During the Byzantine period, Kos was part of the *theme* of the Dodecanese and, like the other islands, was the object of repeated attacks by pirates. In AD 553, a large earthquake shook the island, leaving nothing but ruins in its wake, and Kos fell into obscurity for several years.

In AD 1204, the Franks dissolved the Byzantine empire, after capturing its capital, Constantinople, and proceeded to make themselves masters of the Aegean. Kos became a duchy of the Venetian republic until 1262, when it was liberated by Michael Palaiologos and annexed once more to the Byzantine empire. In 1302 it was captured by the Venetians and in 1304 by the Genoese, falling in 1314 to

The Soroco castle outside Antimacheia.

the Knights of the Order of St John, whose headquarters was on Rhodes. The Knights organised the army and the fleet and saw to it that the island was defended by major fortification works. In 1457, after Constantinople had already fallen to the Ottoman Turks (1453), the islanders vigorously resisted a Turkish attack and, defended by their strong Venetian fortifications, succeeded in repelling the enemy. After repeated attacks, the Turks ultimately wore down the resistance of the people of Kos and captured the island, along with the rest of the Dodecanese, in 1522. The period of subjugation by the Turks plunged the island into obscurity and darkness for almost 400 years, until 1912.

In 1912, Kos, like the rest of the Dodecanese, was occupied by the Italians. It was captured by the Germans in October 1943, and experienced the nightmare of Nazi occupation. After the defeat of Germany and the retreat of the German armies (1945), a British military administration was established on the island until March 1948, when, with the signing of the Treaty of Paris, the islands were incorporated into the Greek state. Since that date, Kos and the other islands have shared the destiny of Greece and her struggles for progress and prosperity.

Above: area of the harbour excavation. The sanctuary of Aphrodite. Right: the Odeon.

HIPPOKRATES, THE GREAT PHILOSOPHER - DOCTOR

Hippokrates is the most famous son of Kos, and still represents an important chapter in the island's history. He was born in 460 BC and died far from his birthplace, in Thessaly, in 357 BC (in 375 or 377 BC, according to other views). He was the son of Phainarete, who was descended from the mythical hero Herakles, and the doctor Gnosidikos, his first teacher in medicine. He studied at the Asklepieion on Knidos and completed his education under various philosophers of the period, continually seeking for new knowledge. It is generally agreed that he was a famous doctor, the most distinguished in the ancient world, and the founder of the science of medicine. Though he was a great traveller, the bigger part of Hippokrates' activity was carried out on his native island of Kos, where his school acquired great fame. In 430 BC, during the Peloponnesian War, he was invited to Athens by Perikles and saved the population from the deadly plague. To honour him, the Athenians proclaimed him an Athenian citizen and granted the right of *isopoliteia* (equal civic rights) to his fellow Koans. As a doctor, he offered his services and knowledge of medicine to many other cities, fighting epidemics, curing physical and mental illnesses, teaching, and generally supporting his suffering fellow man. He made an enormous contribution to the development of medicine and marks a landmark in the history of the science. He was the first to distinguish between medicine and religion or magic, and laid the foundations for scientific medical investigation. The rationalism that was one of his characteristic qualities enabled him, despite the rudimentary state of medical knowledge in his time, to make some astonishing observations, the value of which is still acknowledged today.

Part of the harbour excavations.
In the background can be seen the Loggia, a building of 1786, with its elegant minaret.

The principles of Hippokrates were set out in the treatise `Aphorisms', a work which for two millennia - until the end of the 18th century - was regarded as the basic text of medicine.

Several books said to be written by Hippokrates were printed for the first time in 1526 by Aldus Manutius. Some of them, such as the `Concerning air, water and places' and `Concerning the sacred disease' are, quite independently of their scientific value, regarded as important sources for ancient Greek prose.

Apart from all else, Hippokrates was also the inventor of the code of ethics of the medical profession, through the Hippokratic oath, in which he lucidly defined his mission and the duties of the doctor. The following is a free translation of the oath sworn by the pupils of Hippokrates:

THE HIPPOKRATIC OATH
(sworn by the pupils of Hippokrates)

'I swear by Apollo the healer, and by Asklepios and the goddesses Hygeia and Panakeia, and I call to witness all the other gods and goddesses that, according to my ability and judgement, I will observe this oath and agreement: I will hold my teacher in this art equal to my parents and a partner in my livelihood; I will respect him as is befitting, and I will not distinguish between his male children and my brothers, and I will teach them the art, if they so desire, without pay and without any other special agreement. I will teach the preliminary and the special lessons, and in general all my medical knowledge, only to my sons, and to the sons of my teacher, and to my pupils, having first made them swear the oath, and to no other.

I will use treatment for the good of the sick, according to my ability and judgement, avoiding all harm and wrong-doing. I will give no one deadly poison, even if they seek it, nor will I recommend such a cure. Similarly, I will give no woman a pessary to induce abortion. I will keep my life and my art pure and unsullied. I will not operate on those suffering from stone, but will leave this to the skilled and experienced therein.

Whatever houses I will visit, I will enter for the good of the sick, and will abstain from any deliberate wrong-doing or harm, and any kind of sexual operation on the female or male body, whether free or slave.

And whatever I learn during the time that I am conducting the treatment, as well as during my daily dealings with men, if it be improper to publish this abroad, I will keep silence, considering it to be confidential.

If I observe this oath and do not violate it, may I succeed in my life and my art, so that all men may always honour me. But if I violate the oath and forswear myself, may all the opposite befall me.'

From Kos Archaeological Museum.
Left: statue of Hygeia with Eros-Hypnos.
Right: statue of Hippokrates.

HIPPOKRATES

POPULAR CULTURE AND TRADITION

Despite the rapid progress made by tourism on the island in recent decades, Kos has retained its popular, traditional character largely unspoiled, especially in the country villages of the interior, which are still far from the noise and bustle of the tourist track. The traditional customs are proudly preserved by the locals and revived at every opportunity, through the festivals held on the feast days of Saints, or at weddings and gatherings of every kind. Here one can enjoy authentic local dances, traditional music and songs, and folk costumes.

Considerable efforts are being made by local cultural groups to preserve the valuable features of the popular tradition of the island.

A few examples of traditional architecture are also preserved in some of the villages, such as Antimacheia, Pyli and others. The House of Antimacheia and the traditional house of Kephalos are open to the public and give a rounded picture of the functioning of the old country household on the island. A few of the inhabitants are still engaged in traditional occupations, such as the ancient art of pottery-making at Kardamaina, and textile-weaving at Asphendiou.

Examples of traditional architecture.

HOBIE CAT

MODERN LIFE ON THE ISLAND

Kos has all the amenities of a cosmopolitan holiday resort.

In the city, there are restaurants of all classes, serving Greek and foreign cuisines, as well as pizzerias, fast-food outlets, patisseries, cafés... And in the coastal villages there are many fish-restaurants offering fresh fish and sea-food, while in the villages in the interior of the island, you will find small tavernas offering Greek *mezedes* (titbits), grill-restaurants, etc.

The island has a lively night-life. There are discotheques, ballrooms in the large hotels, night-clubs, piano-bars, pubs, as well as clubs offering bouzouki and Greek music, programmes of folk-music, etc.

Kos is a paradise for sports-lovers. Facilities for water sports, for which equipment can be rented, are to be found on almost all the beaches on the island and at the large hotel complexes. There are also tennis, volley-ball and basket-ball courts and football pitches.

The port of Kos has facilities for supplying yachts with fuel and water, and there are also health and port authorities there.

Those who would like to take something with them from the island to remind them of their wonderful holiday will be glad to learn that there are, both in the city of Kos and the villages visited by tourists, establishments selling items of folk art, souvenirs, gold-work and very fine jewellery, as well shops at which local products, such as wine, honey, cheese, etc., can be bought.

The island pulsates with life and movement during the high season, when

The joys of the sea and night-life in cosmopolitan Kos.

aeroplanes land one after the other at the busy airport, and boats throng the port. At the same time, visitors throng the hotels, rented rooms, camping sites, beaches and streets... Why not enjoy the beauty and archaeological treasures of Kos some other season? Off-season Kos is more peaceful and more authentic!

CHANGING
ROOM

TOUR OF THE ISLAND

Our tour of the island begins at the north-east end, at the capital of the island, also called Kos.

From here we shall follow the main road, the backbone of the island, running its entire length and taking us to the beautiful villages of the interior. Side roads will lead us to places of archaeological interest and to superb beaches and fishing villages.

Kos has an excellent road network, and there are frequent public transport links between the city and most of the villages of the interior and the beaches. It is possible to rent cars, motor-cycles, and bicycles, and there are many taxis available for hire. So, even if you don't bring your own car with you on one of the regular ferry-boats, you won't find it difficult to move about, and you'll be able to choose whatever means of transport you want to visit the sights of the island.

THE MODERN CITY

The capital and main port, Kos, is located at the north-east end of the island, on a site that has not ceased to be inhabited since the Mycenaean period, as is clear from the finds of the extensive excavations. The city was destroyed by a violent earthquake in 1933, during the Italian occupation. The Italians reconstructed the capital virtually from the foundations, to designs based on Italian models of urban planning. It is to them that are owed the proper road-grid, with wide streets flanked by thick rows of trees, spacious squares, and above all the characteristic, Italian-style houses that stand out amongst the modern apartment buildings and the medieval structures. The variety of the architecture gives the city of Kos its own special colour, in which the contrasts hold surprises in store for the visitors, encouraging them to explore the city step by step in order to discover its hidden treasures. And they will certainly find many of these... Old corners, where one feels one is living a century back in time, modern blocks with shops, places of entertainment and hotels, wide avenues with palm-trees, narrow alleys with small shops selling souvenirs and post-cards, and amidst all this, a large number of buildings in which Venetian elements are to be found side by side with Muslim features, Italian with modern. The most important archaeological sites on the island are the ones

Left: Kos. The harbour.
Below: the market building in the city.

KOSTAKIS
STEFAMAR

scattered throughout the living city, so that to stroll in it gives one a feeling of travelling in time. Romantic bike-rides - the bicycle being the ideal, and usual, means of transport in the streets of Kos - swimming at the nearby beaches, which offer everyone the chance to take part in water-sports, browsing in the shops, a meal in one of the many restaurants, entertainment in the night-clubs in the city - these are some of the choices available to the visitor.

Right: There is a strong Italian element in the architecture of the city.
Right: the harbour.

IDEAL

THE ANCIENT CITY

In the 6th century BC, the population of Kos was concentrated at the south-west end of the island, where the city of Astypalaia had been founded, on the site of the modern Kephalos. Remains of this first capital, which continued to exist for the following two centuries, are preserved at Palatia. A devastating earthquake in the 4th century BC levelled Astypalaia, and the inhabitants decided to found a new city, this time on the north-east coast of the island, on a site that had been continuously occupied since the Mycenaean period. The foundations of the new city, Kos, were laid in 366 BC, according to the archaeologists. The finds indicate that it was quite extensive, with a circuit of about 4 kilometres, and had an advanced water-supply and drainage system, strong fortifications, a well-laid out street-grid, a fortified harbour, notable buildings, sanctuaries, gymnasia, an Odeon, etc. All these demonstrate that the city was a well-organised, flourishing state that reached the height of its power and prosperity in the 4th century BC. Many of the finds from the excavations are displayed in the interesting archaeological museum in the city. The ruins of ancient Kos are divided into four excavation sectors, which will be separately described. These are: harbour excavations, the sector near the port, the west excavations, in the west part of the city, and the central and eastern excavations.

a) The harbour excavations

The major earthquake of 1933 shook the island and levelled many buildings in the city, and several ruined buildings of the ancient capital have been discovered beneath

Area of the harbour excavations.
Right: ruins of the ancient agora.
Below: restored columns of the east stoa.

Statues from Kos Archaeological Museum.
Right: the goddess Artemis.
Discovered in the 'House of Europa'.

the debris. Amongst these may be distinguished parts of the ancient 4th century BC defence wall, which is 6-8 metres thick and ran down to the harbour. A very small temple of the 3rd century BC has also been found; it was probably dedicated to the mythical hero Herakles, whose activity was linked with the island of Kos. Exquisitely decorated mosaics dating from the 3rd century AD have been discovered near his sanctuary. Other important finds from the excavation of the harbour include the ruins of the ancient agora, dating from the 4th-3rd centuries BC, with two majestic columns supporting an arch. The Aphrodision, or sanctuary of Pandemos and Aphrodite Pontia, of the 2nd century BC, is a 'twin' sanctuary, with one of the two small temples dedicated to Pandemos and the other to Aphrodite Pontia. The latter was a typical temple of its period, though today only a few architectural members survive. The east stoa of the agora, dating from the 4th or the 3rd century BC, was the most important and earliest structure in this area; eight columns of it have been restored. Some of the finds from the stoa are on display in the archaeological museum of the city.

A three-aisled basilica was built on the ruins, in the 4th or 5th century AD - an odd, but by no means unusual practice - the foundations of which are preserved around the restored columns. Next to it can be seen a

cruciform font, which belonged to the church, while a short distance away are the remains of a small Hellenistic sanctuary.

b) West excavations

Most of the ruins belong to this sector.

Two ancient paved streets have been discovered crossing the archaeological site at right angles to each other. One ran next to the *xysto* (an indoor running track and training area), which was an imposing building with 81 columns, of which 17 have been restored. On the same site were found Mycenaean remains and a geometric tomb. Near the *xysto* is the west bath-house, part of the vaulted room of which is still preserved. There is another baths in the harbour, with the ruins of a circular room and stoas, and also the north baths, in the area of which an important inscription was discovered. All these bath-houses are Roman buildings.

A large mosaic of the 2nd century AD has been discovered near the west baths, with scenes of men wrestling with animals, and depictions of Apollo, the Muses and Paris. There are also remains of two early Christian basilicas in the area of the west bath-house. Opposite is the Nymphaion, or *forica*, as it was called by the Romans who built it. This is an elegant 3rd century AD building, which was originally thought to be a sanctuary of the nymphs - whence its name;

Right: the Odeon.
Below: the 'Xysto'.

it was later discovered that it was a Roman public latrine. Eleven of its columns have been restored, and it has a paved courtyard with mosaics, while a drainage system can also be made out. There are recesses for basins on one side, and the interior walls are revetted with coloured marble. The ruins are also preserved of the ancient stadium (2nd century BC), where the starting point for the races can be seen. The stadium is reckoned to have been 180 metres long and 30 metres wide.

Opposite the *xysto* stands the well-preserved Roman Odeon, a building of the 2nd century AD. The auditorium is preserved, with 9 rows of seats, which have been restored, and also the orchestra, part of the floor of the *proskenion* and the *paraskenion*, and a number of vaulted rooms, in which were found many interesting sculptures, now on display in the archaeological museum of Kos. Mention may be made, finally, of the small Roman house dubbed the 'House of Europa' by the archaeologists, after the famous mosaic floor dating from the 3rd century AD found in one of its small rooms. The mosaic depicts Europa sitting on a bull. In other rooms in this house have been found wall-paintings with a variety of subjects drawn from myth, and statues, which are on display in the archaeological museum of the city (Dionysos group, Asklepios, Artemis, Hygeia, and Hermes resting on a rock).

Finally, a road leads from the Odeon to the church of Ayios Ioannis Prodromos '*ta epta vimata*' (St John the Baptist 'the seven steps'), constructed from ancient architectural members, which is the largest basilica on the island. The well-preserved early Christian baptistery is now used as a cemetery church.

c) Central excavations

Left: Casa Romana
Right: mosaics of superb art.
Top right: Hippokrates and a Koan welcome Asklepios.
Bottom right: the famous 'Abduction of Europa'.

The most important of the ruins in this area is the Roman house (*Casa Romana*) discovered by Laurenzi in 1933 and restored by the Italians, who then ruled the island. This is a Roman villa in the Pompeian style, built on the ruins of a Hellenistic house at the beginning of the 3rd century AD, with outstanding mosaics. It comprises 36 rooms, most of which are adorned with mosaic floors and wall-paintings. There are also three interior courtyards - atria - with decorative cisterns. In the first atrium there is a fountain and a mosaic floor with scenes of wild animals. In a room next to it was found a superb mosaic with a scene of fish in the sea, which is now on display in the museum. In the second atrium there is a mosaic around the cistern with scenes of dolphins and a Nereid crossing the sea on the back of a horse, and two restored columns. The remains that have been discovered suggest that the walls around the atrium were revetted with marble. The third, largest atrium was surrounded by a Rhodian stoa, which had a double colonnade with Ionic and Corinthian columns. Wall-paintings and mosaic floors were found in the rooms next to this atrium.

In the grounds of the *Casa Romana* are the remains of the main bath-house, the baths of the almond-tree as it has been called

by the archaeologists, and a short distance away, is the altar of Dionysos, dating from the 3rd or 2nd century BC and made entirely of marble. A Mycenaean settlement has also been uncovered in this area, together with remains from the geometric period and early Christian finds. The statuettes and bronze objects are amongst the more notable finds, as are the mosaic floors of an ancient house dating from the 2nd or 3rd century AD, with a depiction of Hippokrates, animals fighting, etc. The courtyard of a building has also been found with a reservoir and several mosaics of different periods. One of the best-preserved, which belongs to the 3rd century AD, depicts a leopard and various kinds of fish.

d) East excavations

Several mosaics from the floors of houses have been discovered in this sector. The most impressive are those belonging to a 4th century AD villa, depicting Poseidon, the god of the sea, wrestling with the mythical giant Polybotes. Others show Orpheus playing the kithara and scenes from the animal kingdom. The majority of these superb mosaics have been taken to the Palace of the Grand Master on Rhodes.

Left: the altar of Dionysos.
Right: the sculptural group with Dionysos found in the 'House of Europa'. Kos Archaeological Museum.

THE MEDIEVAL CITY

The medieval city was more limited in area than the ancient, and is located near the harbour. It was surrounded by fortification walls, built by the Knights of St John between 1391 and 1396 to protect the city against the attacks of the Turks. The fortifications were not as strong and well-built as those of other medieval cities, however. The loopholes in the turrets can be seen, and the gate with the coat-of-arms of the Grand Master de Heredia, and also that of Schzegelholz, the governor of Kos. There is also an impressive circular tower on the north-west side of the walls. A short distance away is the *Porta tou Phorou* ('gate of the tax') - as one of the gates is known - which leads to the area of Hippokrates' plane-tree and the castle of the Knights. Entrance to the castle is gained by way of a bridge at right angles to the avenue with the palm-trees. In the medieval period, the modern avenue was a deep moat encircling the castle to guarantee its security. On the other side of the bridge is Hippokrates' plane-tree.

Right: the 'Porta tou Phorou'.
Below: the Government Building.

The Castle (Castello)

The Castle was built on the ruins of ancient fortifications by the Knights of St John, who were masters of the island, at the end of the 14th century. It is in a very good state of preservation and is an example of a technically imposing defence work.

Several architectural members from ancient and Byzantine buildings were used in its construction, and can be seen incorporated in its massive walls. It stands at the entrance to the harbour, a site chosen to defend the city from the frequent attacks on it from the sea. There is a superb view from this point over the sea and the entire city. The Castle is girt by two enclosure walls for greater security. The outer wall has four round bastions at its four corners, and the inner one has four round towers. The gates of the castle are decorated with ancient marble reliefs, and slabs incorporated into the walls are carved with the coats-of-arms of the Grand Masters of the Order of St John and dates. The main gate is flanked by marble pilasters and has a lintel with three escutcheons. Inside the inner courtyard are the west curtain-wall and two stout towers. A room in the castle houses architectural members, inscribed stelai, altars, column capitals, etc.

Views of the city of Kos from the castle.

HIPPOKRATES' PLANE-TREE

The plane-tree stands in the square of the same name (Plateia Platanou). According to tradition, it was under this plane-tree that the great Hippokrates taught and tended the sick. It is an imposing tree with a trunk some 12 metres round, rich foliage and stout branches, supported on columns. Nearby is a spring that supplied water to the Lodge opposite, and a sarcophagus with an inscription carved on it.

Left: the famous plane-tree of Hippokrates. Below: the Loggia.

There are many old churches scattered throughout the city and its environs. The most important amongst them are: the Panayia Gorgoepikoos, Ayios Ioannis Baptistis, Ayios Ioannis Naukleros the neomartyr, Ayios Konstantinos, the Panayia Katevati, Ayia Ekaterini and the Panayia Tsoukalaria. In the city there are also several building remains dating from the Turkish occupation. The most important of these are: the Mosque of the Gazi Hasan Pasha, or Loggia Mosque, built with architectural members from the ancient city. It is an imposing two-storey structure with an elegant minaret, and was built in 1786. The Mosques of the Defterdars, Marouk and Atik, and the mausoleum of Hadji Pasha.

THE MUSEUM

The archaeological museum of Kos, which is located in Plateia Eleftherias, opposite the *Porta tou Phorou* is housed in a fine two-storey building. Telephone: 28.326.

It contains mainly sculptures, mosaics and grave stelai from excavations on the island, most of which date from the Hellenistic and Roman periods.

The most important objects on display are: a portrait statue of Hippokrates found in the Odeon, which belongs to the late Hellenistic period. A statue of Hygeia offering an egg to a snake, with the figure of Eros-Hypnos at her feet, of the 2nd century AD. A funerary statue of an athlete with a victory wreath in his hands, of the 3rd century BC. A headless statue of a woman with superb clothing, found in the ancient Odeon and dating from the Hellenistic period. A statue of Demeter (4th century BC) and a statuette of Kore (3rd century BC), from the sanctuary of Demeter at Kyparissi Amaniou. A headless statue of Asklepios, of the 2nd century BC. A Hellenistic statue of Herakles hunting the Stymphalian Birds. Part of an Archaic relief depicting a boy with a cock (6th century BC). A sculptural group from the 'House of Europa', depicting Dionysos, a satyr and Pan, with a small Eros sitting at Dionysos's feet (2nd century AD). A copy of a statue of the goddess Athena, of the late Hellenistic period.

There are also a large number of mosaics on display in the museum, including the one

Right: Hermes resting.
Kos Archaeological Museum.
Below: Relief depicting a lion.

Kos Archaeological Museum.
Left: Asklepios
Right: headless statue of Aphrodite with the young Eros.

depicting Asklepios being welcomed by a Koan citizen and Hippokrates (2nd or 3rd century AD). Also the mosaic from the Roman house with scenes of fish.

THE ASKLEPIEION

The Asklepieion lies 4 kilometres to the south of the city of Kos, on a hill surrounded by pine trees and cypresses, and is the most important monument on the island. Information: tel: 28.763

The Asklepieion was a sanctuary dedicated to Asklepios, the god of medicine, and had rooms that were used as sanatoria. Construction of it began in the 4th century BC, after the death of Hippokrates. It acquired great fame throughout Greece, thanks to the tradition begun on the island by Hippokrates and continued by his pupils. The sick flocked from everywhere in search of a cure. The sanctuary was also a place of asylum for anyone who was being persecuted. The site was carefully chosen for its healthy climate and water, and there is an enchanting view of the trees around it and the sea in the distance.

The earthquake of 155 BC caused severe damage to the buildings, and that of 554 AD levelled them, though the sanctuary had already begun to decline after the general adoption of Christianity on the island.

Left: the Asklepieion, the first terrace.
Below: the temple of Apollo.

The Asklepieion was excavated at the beginning of the century. Iakovos Zaraphtis, a local antiquarian, had studied the question for years and had gathered together evidence that allowed him to indicate its probable site. The German archaeologist Herzog received a permit from the Turks and began to excavate. During the work, however, he removed some of the finds, which were taken via Constantinople to Berlin.

Because of the sloping terrain, the buildings are erected on three different levels - terraces - which are connected by staircases, now restored.

Left: the Ionic temple of Asklepios.
Below: the large Doric temple of Asklepios.

The first terrace, which probably housed the medical school and the sanatoria, contained the entrance staircase, with 24 steps, the propylaia, statue bases, Roman bath-houses, a stoa, a room for the sick, a toilet, a wall with recesses in which there were statues - a stone representation of Pan was found in one of them - a small temple dedicated by Xenophon, and a second staircase. To the east of the bath-house, the Italians built a small store-room to house the finds.

A staircase leads to the second terrace, on which are to be found the altar of Asklepios or Apollo Kyparissios, of the 4th century BC, the Ionic temple of Asklepios, of the 3rd century BC, the Corinthian temple of Apollo, of the 2nd century BC, the *lesche*, or club-house, a semicircular exedra, the houses of the priests, and a retaining wall. Ascending the steps of a staircase, the

visitor reaches the third terrace. Here are the large Doric temple of Asklepios, dating from the 2nd century BC, the ruins of a Hellenistic stoa that enclosed the area on three sides, and rooms for the sick. From the third terrace, there is an impressive view of the entire archaeological site and the tranquil natural surroundings, and it is easy to understand the sense of grandeur, mystery and confidence that it inspired.

A short distance away from the archaeological site is the building of the International Hippokratic Foundation of Kos. It contains a conference room, scientific laboratories, a well-stocked library, offices, a guest-house and a restaurant. The aims of the foundation include facilitating contact between researchers in the field of medicine, publicising the results of research, organising international medical conferences, awarding prizes for medical writing and discoveries, etc.

AROUND THE TOWN

There are many beautiful locations and excursions in the environs of the city of Kos: the Vourinna spring, or Spring of Hippokrates, is in an idyllic setting just outside the city in the foothills of Mount Dikaios. The spring, which is inside a vaulted Hellenistic building, has been supplying the water needs of the city for 3,000 years. Platani, 2 kilometres to the west of the city, near the International Hippokratic Foundation, is a village with several small restaurants, including the *Ambavris*, the *Kako Prinari*, and the *Paradeisi*. There are also fine beaches to the east, in the direction of Psalidi. The remains of an early Christian three-aisled basilica dedicated to St Gabriel have been discovered in this area. Further to the south is Ayios Phokas beach (8 kilometres south-east of Kos), a major tourist complex, with an excellent beach, fine sea-

bathing, hotels, restaurants and tavernas, night clubs etc. The remains of 'Pelasgian' walls have been discovered in this area. One kilometre to the south-west is the spa, with a superb beach, where there are healing springs, with basins. The waters are recommended for rheumatism and arthritis, and for gynaecological problems. There are more beautiful beaches to the north-west of the city, in the direction of the Skandari promontory, and at Lambi some of the old windmills are preserved, which transport us back through time.

Ayios Phokas.

ASPHENDIOU
Zia - Lagoudi - Zipari

Asphendiou, 14 kilometres to the south of the city, is a traditional Mediterranean village with its houses scattered in the foothills of Mount Dikaios. On one of the peaks of the mountain is the chapel of Christ the Saviour, or Christ the Just (Dikaios), which was built in 1079. The surrounding settlements include Ayios Dimitrios and Khaikhoutes, the beautiful village of Zia, built on a hill with a superb view of the sea and lush vegetation, Lagoudi, with the church of Ayios Ioannis Theologos (St John the Theologian) built amidst the rocks, and Asomatos, with the church of the Asomatoi, which dates from the 11th century and has a fine iconostasis. A short distance away is Linopotis, and Zipari in the plain. Outside this village were found the remains of two early Christian basilicas.

Top left: Lagoudi.
Bottom left: Zia.
Below: Lambi.

PYLI
Amaniou - Marmari - Tingaki

Pyli: this village is in the heart of the island, 17 kilometres south-west of the city. A beautiful traditional settlement built amidst olive groves, it is a lively and interesting centre. Near the square there is a picturesque fountain with six spouts, and next to it the ancient vaults that, according to

Left: Pyli.
Right: the beautiful beach at Tingaki.

tradition, are associated with the early king Charmylos. The king's tomb is in the same area - a semicircular building with twelve identical crypts. Above the tomb stands the chapel of the Cross. The pieces of white marble incorporated into the masonry of this building are parts of the columns of the Ionic temple that enclosed the facade of Charmylos's tomb. Fourteen kilometres to the east, in the foothills of Mount Dikaios, are the ruins of Palio Pylio, a village abandoned by its inhabitants in the 18th century because of a cholera epidemic. The remains of a castle are preserved on a height overlooking the ruins of the village. In the old village can be found the church of the Archon Michael, and the notable church of the Presentation in the Temple; the latter has a wood-carved iconostasis, 14th century wall-paintings, and ancient columns, probably from the sanctuary of the goddess Demeter, the ruins of which have been found at Kyparissi Amaniou. Many of the very important finds from this archaeological site are on display in the museum of Kos. A short distance to the north is the coastal settlement of Marmari, which has a large beach, very good sea-bathing, and many tourist amenities. On the same coast lies the busy holiday centre of Tingaki, which belongs to the community of Asphendiou and has one of the best beaches on the island.

ANTIMACHEIA
Kastro - Mastichari - Plaka

Antimacheia lies 23 kilometres to the south-west of Kos, near the airport. It is a picturesque traditional village, whose inhabitants respect and preserve the customs and traditions of their native place. They love to dance and sing, and eat good food, and keep alive their traditional music, which can be enjoyed at the local festivals, when the versifiers, singers, musicians and dancers of Antimacheia let their hair down. It is well worth visiting the House of Antimacheia, a typical traditional house of the beginning of the present century, built on the initiative of the Cultural Society, and containing furniture, objects, vessels and tools gleaned from old houses in the village. The layout is that of a typical local traditional house and, in addition to the main residence, it has a barnyard with farming tools, the *fournario* with the loom, a courtyard with the *stamnostati* and stables for the animals. In front of the house is the priest's mill, which has been restored and is in operation. On a hill three kilometres to the east of the village stands the Venetian castle. Its fortifications are preserved in fairly good condition, and in the interior are the remains of houses, water cisterns, and two old churches - the ruined church of Ayios Nikolaos, and that of Ayia Paraskevi, which is in better condition. The picturesque windmills in this area give the landscape a romantic touch.

Right: one of the picturesque churches of Kos.
Below: Mastichari.

WATER SPORTS
CAPT PETA

A metalled road leads to Mastichari, the harbour of Antimacheia, 4 kilometres to the north of the village. This is a tourist resort, with a large sandy beach and many tourist amenities. To the west is Ayios Ioannis beach, an excellent beach with superb sea-bathing. In this area was found the early Christian three-aisled basilica of St John, with a mosaic floor and a fine baptistery.

To the south of Antimacheia is Plaka, a beautiful site set deep amidst virgin nature, with verdant vegetation and abundant water. It has been laid out as a picnic area, with wooden benches and tables that can be used by day-trippers during their tour of the natural beauty spots of the island.

KARDAMAINA

Kardamaina is 29 kilometres from the city, on the south-east coast of the island. It is a summer resort with large hotel complexes, rooms for rent, restaurants, bars, discos and, in general, all the features of an attractive tourist centre. It draws large numbers of summer visitors, who enjoy the sun and sea, the fresh fish and locally grown fruit and vegetables, and also the modern residential facilities. On a hill just outside the village are preserved the remains of a castle, around which the old settlement grew up. There are also the foundations of a Byzantine church in the area, and the remains of a Hellenistic theatre and tomb.

The long beach at Kardamaina.

This is thought to have been the site of the ancient city of Halassarna, which had a large temple dedicated to the god Apollo. At Kardamaina there are pottery workshops at which fine hand-made pottery can be purchased. The nearby island of Nisyros can be visited from the small harbour.

KEPHALOS
Kamari - Ayios Stephanos - Limionas

Kephalos is at the south-west end of the island, 45 kilometres from the capital. It is at the end of the main road artery that runs across the island from Kos. The village stands a short distance from the sea, on a hill with the picturesque windmill of Papavasilis on the summit. The dense buildings and narrow streets give the settlement the character of a typical island village. It has deep traditions, a rich history and great archaeological interest, for the ancient capital of the island, Astypalaia, was in this area. In the village itself, it is worth visiting the traditional house of Kephalos, which serves as a museum, housing typical objects associated with the agricultural life of the island.

One kilometre away is its harbour, Kamari, which has a long beach, tourist accommodation, facilities for water-sports,

Right: the small island of Kastri in Kephalos Bay.
Below: the beach at Kamari.

tavernas, etc. The small island of Kastri, with its picturesque church, lies off the open bay of Kephalos. To the north-east are the superb beaches of Chrysi Akti, Paradeisos, Kambos, and Ayios Stephanos, with their unique sands and limpid sea. The ruins were found here of an early Christian basilica dedicated to Ayios Stephanos, with fine mosaics and columns. At Palatia, two kilometres to the west of Kephalos, are preserved the remains of the ancient capital of the island, Astypalaia, which was levelled by a devastating earthquake. The foundations of a temple and the remains of a theatre have been uncovered. Beyond Palatia, in the direction of Zini, is Aspri Petra, a prehistoric cave in which neolithic remains have been excavated. Other sites in this area include the church of the Panayia Palatiani, built on a hill near Palatia, with a superb view, that of the Panayia Ziniotissa, on the slopes of Mount Zini, and the monastery of St John, 7 kilometres to the south, set in a magnificent natural location, with the barren island of Yali lying to the east. To the north is the naturally protected harbour of Limionas.

Left: the basilica of Ayios Stephanos.
Below: Paradeisos beach.

GENERAL INFORMATION

HOW TO GET THERE

Kos is linked by air with Athens and Rhodes. The airport is 27 kilometres from the city.

There is a ferry-boat service from Piraeus (200 nautical miles).

LOCAL CONNECTIONS

Kos also has ferry connections with the rest of the Dodecanese, some of the Cyclades, the islands of the east Aegean, Kavala, Thessaloniki and Crete. **There are daily services to Nisyros from Kardamaina and Kephalos.** During the summer

months, many tourist vessels also make trips to Nisyros, Pserimos and Kalymnos.

Kos is connected by express boats with several of the islands in the Dodecanese and the east Aegean.

PUBLIC TRANSPORT

The island has, generally speaking a good road network, and there are frequent road services. The local bus-company (KTEL) runs daily services to Zipari-Asphendiou-Tingaki-Pyli-Kardamaina-Mastichari-Kephalos.

There are also many meter-taxis and offices renting cars, motor bicycles and bicycles.

TOURIST OFFICES

There are many tourist offices in the city, and several in places that have a sizeable tourist trade. They organise excursions to all the sights and places of archaeological interest on the island, and boat trips to nearby destinations.

ENTERTAINMENT SPORT - ACTIVITIES

The city of Kos, and the coastal villages visited by tourists all have restaurants of all classes, serving Greek and international cuisines, ouzo-bars with local *mezedes* (titbits), cafés, patisseries, tavernas, pizzerias, etc. For night life, there are discos, bars, pubs, centres with folk and island music, etc. There are also several open-air cinemas.

Every kind of water-sport can be enjoyed on Kos, and it is possible to rent canoes, water-bikes, and wind-surfing and other equipment.

In the large hotels, there are facilities for tennis and mini-golf. There are also public football pitches and volley-ball and basket-ball courts.

The port of Kos has a facility for refuelling yachts, and there are customs and health authorities.

LOCAL EVENTS - FESTIVALS

Many festivals and traditional celebrations take place in the city of Kos and the villages.

Kos: the Hippokrateia, in August, is a festival which includes exhibitions, theatrical performances, local dances, etc.

The Asklepieion: there is a re-enactment of the `Hippocratic Oath', every Sunday afternoon during the summer.

Antimacheia: the festivals of the Holy Trinity, the Holy Apostles (30th June), the Virgin (15 August), St Niketas (15 September), with folk dances and local musicians. Food and wine are provided at several of these.
There is a traditional carnival with spontaneous good humour and fancy dress.

Mastichari: the festival of St. John on 29 August.

Kardamaina: major festival of St John (29 August), and the Birth of the Virgin (8 September).

Kephalos: the festivals of St Paraskevi on 26 June, St John on 29 August, the Virgin on 15 August, at which food is provided by the stock-breeders of the area. A traditional carnival. Athletic events in the middle of May, and the `Tour of Kephalos' in October.

Pyli-Marmari: the festival of St George (23 April), wine and *mezedes*, and horse-races. On 23 June of Ay-Yanni; the custom of the fortune-telling, and the `silent water'. In the square at Pyli there is a parade of floats during carnival, and satirical couplets are recited, inspired by everyday events in the life of the village. Cultural events are also held in August.

USEFUL TELEPHONE NUMBERS -KOS (0242)

Tourist Police	22.444
Port Authority	26.594
Municipal Offices	22.326
Telephone Company (OTE)	22.499
Hospital	22.300
TAXI	23.333

USEFUL TELEPHONE NUMBERS - NISYROS (0242)

Police	31.201
Municipal Offices	31.222
Community Clinic	31.217
Therapeutic springs	31.011
Telephone Company (OTE)	31.249

Club

NISYROS

HOW TO GET THERE

Nisyros is connected by ferry with Piraeus and several of the islands in the Dodecanese and the Cyclades. Distance from Piraeus 202 nautical miles. It is at a distance of 8 nautical miles from Kos and there are daily connections.

It is also connected by hydrofoil starting from Rhodes with islands in the Dodecanese.

GEOGRAPHICAL AND HISTORICAL OUTLINE

Nisyros lies between Kos and Tilos, a short distance away from the coast of Turkey.

It is a volcanic island, round in shape, with few bays or inlets in the coast, and has fertile soil and mineral springs.

The highest peak on the island is the Crater (698 metres), a presently inactive volcano. The island has an area of 41 square miles and 28 kilometres of coastline. It was inhabited in antiquity, when it was called Porphyris. According to the mythological tradition, it was connected with Kos in primeval times, and was separated from it by Poseidon.

The island itself is a volcano, and it was created by the intense geological changes caused by the seismic activity in the Mediterranean, which is why mythology considers Nisyros as being linked with The Battle Of The Giants. The story goes that Poseidon broke off a piece of Kos in order to throw it on the giant Polivotis.

When the huge rock covered the giant, he remained in the sea alive and that is how Nisyros was born. The volcano was created by the groans of Polivotis.

LOCAL EVENTS - FESTIVALS

Many local customs are still preserved on Nisyros.

The traditional wedding lasts three days and ends in dancing to folk instruments and singing in the square. There is a large festival on 15 August at the monastery of the Panayia Spiliani.

Left : Map of Nisyros, etching, 17 x 12.25 cm. 1688.
Right : Picturesque street in Mandraki, in the background the derelict castle of Spiliani
Pgs. 116-117: Sunset in Mandraki.

TOUR OF THE ISLAND

The picturesque town of **Mandraki** is the capital and harbour of the island. The characteristic white houses with their flat roofs ascend the rock to the castle on its summit. This is the *castle of Spiliani*, built by the Order of the Knights of St. John and named after the monastery of the *Panayia Spiliani*. Its church is a basilica with a fine 18th c. iconostasis.

The town has a small folklore museum, housed in a traditional building and containing some interesting exhibits. To the north-west is *Palaiokastro*, with the ruins of the ancient city. Near Mandraki there are some therapeutic sulphur springs.

The sea-side settlement of **Pali**, which has a fine beach and plenty of fish, is 4 kilometres south-east of Mandraki.

The mountain village of **Emborios** lies 8 kilometres south-east of Mandraki. A short distance away is the monastery of the *Panayia Kyra*, built on a hill 500 metres high with a panoramic view over the entire island. The ruins of a Venetian castle are preserved at the highest point of the settlement.

Further south is the village of **Nikia** (14 kilometres from Mandraki), which has a notable monastery of *Ayios Ioannis*. The Nisyros **volcano** can be visited from here. The crater has a diameter of 260 metres and is 30 metres deep.

The small island of **Yali**, 4 nautical miles north-west of Nisyros, has a small settlement.

Right, above : Mandraki.
Right, below : The Monastery of Aghiou Ioanni in Nikia.
Below : The seaside resort Pali.
Pgs. 120-121 : The volcano of Nisyros.

ACCOMMODATION - KOS

HOTELS

KOS (CHORA) (0242)

TCAT.	NAME	TEL.	BEDS
A	DAEDALOS	91527	625
A (h-b)	DIMITRA BEACH	22737	261
A (h-b)	KARAVIA BEACH	41291/4	563
A	CONTINENTAL PALACE	22737	393
A	LAKITIRA	91537	396
A (ff)	BRISTOL	22575	42
B	ANGELA	21246	90
B	AYIOS KONSTANDINOS	23301	232
B	AEGEON	24701/2	76
B (p)	ALKYON	23739	42
B	ALEXANDRA	28301/5	150
B (p)	AMERIKANA	22947	26
B (p)	ANNA	23030	34
B p)	ARION	22256	32
B	ARTEMIS	23313	110
B	ASTRON	23705/7	136
B	ATLANTA BEACH	28889	80
B (p)	AFENDOULIS	28301/5	150
B (p)	GALAZIOS OURANOS	22090	20
B (p)	GALLIA	23230	39
B (p)	GEORGIA	28577	18
B	YASEMI	-	34
B (p)	GOLDEN CITY	23057	26
B (p)	ELLAS	23017	36
B	THEOXENIA	22310/2	78
B	IPPOTON	23503/5	78
B	IRIS	24454	57
B	KRIS-MARI	91642/4	165
B	KOS	22480/1	262
B (ff)	KOS SUNSMILE	25607	36
B (p)	KOSTIS	22195	22
B (h-b)	LAND OF ROSES		132
B	MARINA	28726	104
B	MARMARI BEACH	41002	207

CAT.	NAME	TEL.	BEDS
B (p)	MERSINI	22602	20
B (p)	MEROPIS	22789	36
B (p)	OLYMPIA	22812	41
B	OSCAR SEVASTI	28936	42
B	PALLADION BUNGALOWS	41407/9	100
B (p)	PARITSA	28971	100
B	PARK LANE	29170	106
B (ff)	PAULINA	-	44
B	PYLI BAY	41211	209
B	SANDY BEACH	41426	180
B (p)	SEMIRAMIS	-	34
B (p)	SOPHIA	23051/2	17
B (ff)	STADION	21145	20
B (b)	TONIS	41457	78
C	AYIOS GEORGIOS	-	77
C	AGRELLIS	91226	65
C (ff)	ADONIS	-	29
C	CATHERINE	28285	48
C (ff)	AKTAION APARTMENTS	24977	37
C (ff)	ALEXANDRA II	25202	63
C	ALIKI	24198	37
C	ANASTASIA	28598	77
C	ANTHOULA	71339	50
C	ANNETA	24031	42
C (ff)	APOLLONIA	25653	48
C (ff)	ASPA HOLIDAYS	28394	38
C (ff)	ASTERIAS	23665	39
C	VERONIKI	28122/3	36
C	VIRGINIA	23749	42
C	GALAXIAS	23361	42
C	GALINI	23368	60
C	DELFINI	28802	34
C	DIMITRIS PARITSA	24673	80
C	DIETHNES	23751/2	121
C	ELISABETH	22543	32
C	ELLI	28401/2	150

ACCOMMODATION - KOS

CAT.	NAME	TEL.	BEDS
C	ELMA	22920/1	92
C (ff)	ESPERIDES	-	63
C (ff)	EFTYHIA	23212	14
C	ZEUS	23129	71
C	ZEPHYROS	22245	88
C	ZIKAS	28735	36
C	THEONIA	23303	89
C	THOMAS	-	46
C	IVISKOS	22214	25
C	IMPERIAL	23800/2	134
C	HIPPOCRATES	23221	48
C	IREN	28186	68
C	KAMARI BAY	71556	80
C	CAMELIA	28983	42
C	CAPETAN ACHILLEAS	23674	70
C	CAPTAIN'S	22961	52
C	KARIS	22990	54
C (ff)	KENDRO AYIA MARINA	-	161
C	KOALA	22897	81
C	KONI	23913	37
C	KONDIA BEACH	22663	101
C (ff)	KONSTANDIA	28244	28
C (ff)	KONDOVEROS	-	14
C	KOS BAY	26126	103
C	KOSTEL	22968/9	70
C	MANOS	28931	29
C	MARI	22190	39
C	MARITINA	23241/2	132
C	MARITON APARTMENTS	25875	24
C	MESOYIOS	23161	24
C	BAHAMAS	24374	56
C	BRISTOL	22865	71
C (h-b)	NIREIDES BEACH	23380	147
C	OLGA	22694	57
C	OSCAR	28090/1	308
C	PANDELIS	25456/7	93
C	PARADISOS	22988	100
C	PAVLOS	23151	121
C (ff)	POPI	25106	57
C	POSEIDON	23386	67
C	SUNBEAM	91522	19
C (ff)	SOLEIL APARTMENTS	23926	40
C	TITANIA	22556	109

ANTIMACHEIA

CAT.	NAME	TEL.	BEDS
C	THALASSIA AVRA	51501	35

KARDAMAINA

CAT.	NAME	TEL.	BEDS
A	APOLLO'S MUSES	91668	154
A	LANGAS AEGEAN VILLAGE	91401/2	662
A	NORIDA BEACH	91231/2	1029
B	AKTI TO OREO LIMANI	91217	280
B (p)	ALMA	91365	40
B (p)	AVDAVIS	91461	25
B (p)	VILLA PANDAROTA	91134	18
B (p)	ILIOLOUSTI THEA	-	46
B (b)	KARDA BEACH	91332	131
B (ff)	KARMELINA	-	58
B (p)	MARIGO	22544	13
B	RIO	91627	34
B	SARONIS	91513	186
B	SILVER BEACH	91415	80
C (ff)	ANGELIKI	91354	46
C	VALIANAKIS BEACH	91354	142
C (ff)	VARKAS	91517/8	49
C (ff)	VERGINA	-	23
C (ff)	ELGA	-	69
C (ff)	INO	-	43
C (ff)	KALLIA APARTMENTS	-	27
C (ff)	KALOXENIA	-	28

CAT.	NAME	TEL.	BEDS
C	KARDAMENA	91252	30
C	KARDAMOS	91323	124
C	CLEOPATRA	91181/4	85
C (ff)	LYDIA	-	32
C (ff)	MAMOUZELOS	91467	60
C	MIKARTZI	91492	61
C (ff)	NISIA	91091	46
C (ff)	NIKOLIOS	-	41
C	PANORAMA	91256/9	40
C (ff)	PERIVOLI	91105	24
C	SILVER BEACH II	-	39

KEPHALOS

CAT.	NAME	TEL.	BEDS
A	KOS	71565	880
B	KARAVADOS BEACH	69400	70
C	KOKOLAKIS BEACH	71466	44
C	KORDISTOS	71251	50
C	SAKKALIS INN	-	46

LAMBI

CAT.	NAME	TEL.	BEDS
A	ATLANTIS	28731/4	616
B	ATHINA	25044/5	132
B	AEOLOS BEACH	26781/8	238
B	ANGELA BEACH	22800	80
B (H-B)	APELLIS	24629	62
B	APOLLON	22853	152
B	GAYIA	22855	72
B	IKAROS	26611	190
B	CALYPSO	23552	84
B	COLUMBIA BEACH	28440	108
B	COSMOPOLITAN	23411/5	148
B	HOTEL BEACH BLUE SEA	26250	79
C	ALICE SPRINGS	23473	40
C	ARGO	24375	100
C	ATLANTIS II	23755	153
C	CAPTAIN ILIAS	-	39
C	LAURA	23981	47
C	BOHEME	23754	79
C	FROSYNI	25231	97

MARMARI

CAT.	NAME	TEL.	BEDS
A	ANGELA MARE	41922/5	392
B (ff)	YAKALIS	-	90
B	NINA	41590	116
C	BLUE JAY	41533	74
C	HERMES	-	58

MASTICHARI

CAT.	NAME	TEL.	BEDS
A	CANARY BEACH	51099	160
A	NEPTUNE BEACH	51141	475
A (b)	PRINCESS OF KOS BAY	41524/5	320
B (ff)	KARANDONIS	-	70
B (p)	MASTICHARI BEACH	51371	21
B (p)	WAVE	51545	25
C (p)	ARAD	51167/8	23
C (ff)	ARTEMIS II	51161/2	21
C (ff)	LOUIS	-	29

MYDOS LAPA

CAT.	NAME	TEL.	BEDS
C	ALBATROSS BEACH	23381/3	117

TINGAKI

CAT.	NAME	TEL.	BEDS
A	TINGAKI BEACH	29258	309
B	TINGAKI STAR	29541/2	143
B (p)	HOLLYWOOD	29206	38
C (ff)	ARIADNE	-	24
C (ff)	ASPRO SPITI	29296	44
C	VILLA ANDREAS	29221	59
C (ff)	ILIOLOUSTES MERES		

ACCOMMODATION - KOS

CAT.	NAME	TEL.	BEDS
		29091	86
C	KONSTANDINOS ILIOS	29411/2	162
C	MENI BEACH	29217	70
C	PAXINOS	29306	44
C	SUNSET	29428/9	187
C	TROPICAL SOL	29341	96
C	IPINEMA	-	21
PSALIDI			
A	ARCHIPELAGOS	23408	209

CAT.	NAME	TEL.	BEDS
A	IPPOKRATIS PALACE	24401/8	280
A	PLATANISTA	25452	297
A	RAMIRA BEACH	22891/4	500
A	SUN PALACE	24391	274
A	OKEANIS	24641	651
B	THEODOROU BEACH	22280	106
B	PHOENIX BEACH	21771	72
C	GALAZIA LIMNI	-	91
C	ENDMARK	25952	98

CAMPING

KOS CAMPING (Psalidi). Tel.: 23275 and 23910

ACCOMMODATION - NISYROS

CAT.	NAME	TEL.	BEDS
MANDRAKI (0242)			
C	WHITE BEACH	31497/8	91
C	PORFYRIS	31376	73
C	KHARITOS	31322	24
C	MUNICIPAL GUEST - HOUSE	31204	45
NIKIA (0242)			
C	MUNICIPAL GUEST - HOUSE	31401	14

Note: There are also D and E category hotels.
p = pension/noarding house, ff = furnished flats, b = bungalows,
h-b = hotel and bungalows.

KOS - NISYROS

SCALE 1:180.000

- Asphalt-Paved Road
- Non-asphalt Road
- Carriageway
- Castle
- Archaeological Site
- Camping

Korifi
Ak. Roussa
AULOS PSERIMOU
Ak. Ammoudia
Lampi
ORMOS KO
KOS
Livadia
Tigaki
Psalidi
Ak. Louros
Selveri
Dio Eklissies
Ag. Ioannis
Platani
Paradissi
Evagelistria
Messaria
Zipari
Ag. Vassileios
Giapili
ASKLEPION
Panagia
Ag. Georgios
Marmara
Ag. Panteleimon
Linopotis
211
Panagia
Spasmeni Petra
Prof. Ilias
Prof. Ilias
351
Agios
Dimitrios
Drakou Petra
466
Agios Fokas
Trotsouli
Aklafti
Ag. Georgios
Amaniou
Asfendiou
Seladi
Lagoudi
Zia
Apovrisi
Empros Thermi
Ag. Georgios
Mamali
Ag. Zacharias
Oros Dikaios
Panagia
Pal. Pilion
Ag. Ioannis Theologos
Kouvas
Akaki
Pisso Thermi
Panagia Valari
Valari
Kardamena
NISYROS
Akrotiri
Paloi
Ak. Katsouni
Loutra
MANDRAKI
Spiliani
Emporios
Ag. Vassileios
539
698
Prof. Ilias
M. Panagias Kiras
Ak. Skafidot
589
M. Ag. Ioannou Theologou
Nikia
Ag. Marina
Ak. Katero
Argos
Drakospila
Ag. Georgios
Ormos Korfos
Ak. Leukos
Ormos Leukos
Avlaki
Ak. Avlaki
128
STROGYLI
Ak. Kamara
IOS ANTONIOS
Therapeutic Springs
Beach
Anchorage

ENGLISH TRANSLATION: DAVID HARDY

PHOTOGRAPHERS: K. ADAM, V. VOUTSAS,
Y. YIANNELOS, Y. KOUROUPIS

PRINTING: PERGAMOS S.A.